A Bright Forgetting

poems by

Lynne Martin Bowman

Finishing Line Press
Georgetown, Kentucky

A Bright Forgetting

Copyright © 2023 by Lynne Martin Bowman
ISBN 979-8-88838-155-7 First Edition
All rights reserved under International and Pan-American Copyright Conventions. No part of this book may be reproduced in any manner whatsoever without written permission from the publisher, except in the case of brief quotations embodied in critical articles and reviews.

ACKNOWLEDGMENTS

The author wishes to thank the journals and competitions in which the poems below were honored or have appeared. Some poems appear in chapbook in different form from their original publications.

The Crab Orchard Review: "Yard in Late Winter," "Field in Late Summer"
Crosswinds Poetry Journal: "Countless"
Randall Jarrell Poetry Prize, honorable mention (no publication): "Field in Late Summer"
Fire and Chocolate: "Where My Father is Buried I Have Not Been"
Icarus International: "Bird in the Rain," "Gone to Brightness," "Like Air," "Duende: For Her"
The Mississippi Review: "Domestica"
Petroglyph: "Canyon Tour"
Sonora Review, Poetry Prize Winner: "Plain Song"
Sow's Ear Poetry Review: "Not Yet Easeful"
Tar River Poetry: "That Painful Remembering," "Light Lifting"

Publisher: Leah Huete de Maines
Editor: Christen Kincaid
Cover Art: James H. Bowman Photographer
Author Photo: James H. Bowman Photographer
Cover Design: Elizabeth Maines McCleavy

Order online: www.finishinglinepress.com
also available on amazon.com

Author inquiries and mail orders:
Finishing Line Press
PO Box 1626
Georgetown, Kentucky 40324
USA

Table of Contents

That Painful Remembering 1

Bird in the Rain 2

In Memoriam 3

Where My father is Buried I Have Not Been 4

Grace Confusing 5

Gone to Brightness 6

Like Air 7

To that Pilgrim Sky the Sun Slips 8

Bright Forgetting 9

In the Same Boat 10

Domestica 11

Duende: For Her 13

Light Lifting 15

Countless 16

Looking Up 17

Not Yet Easeful 18

What Trees Remember 19

Field in Late Summer 20

Heard While Still Sleeping 21

Canyon Tour 22

Out of Coeur d'Alene 23

Going into the Grand Canyon 24

Plain Song 25

Where All Things Are Made New 26

Departing 27

For my parents,
Lealon E. Martin (1910-1996) and
Lucile Sissell Martin (1913-2003)

and my husband, Jim:

whose love is everything

That Painful Remembering

It is well known that everything is going away,
somehow we forget and then remember
to say goodbye, even to the gleaming mountain,
washed pink then brown, dissolving into the river.

The world discards everything, even itself—
your old wingtip shoes, your suits and ties, the last
kiss you gave her—swept along with the mountain,
the hills, last year's leaves, the great and ancient forests—
all fall like the whispers of last night when I thought of you.

Sometimes we can't remember, don't want to, will not,
but this regular forgetting is only what is wanted—
memory clouds the terrible country, the roads buckle,
the crenelated castle folds—I do not want a picture of you falling,
hip breaking on the pale grey linoleum. I cannot remember
how long you lay in that dark bathroom before we heard you.

Bird in the Rain

Dancing thinner until it stops
like a river dries, upswings to air,
rain lifts the blue heron
who droops over the sky, ghost
crossing streets and trees as if in prayer.

This is where my father may be going,
a heavy bird needs lifting, skin
no longer fits across the bone,
a lost boy speaks of home, idly crosses
town to walk the river, muddy, dreaming.

He shot sparrow and squirrel,
rough with beebee gun or sling,
just like ten year old grandmother's
walk from fire, Georgia burning, across
a thousand miles with birds for food.

Now wings bend awkward for air,
a small body curls to bed like leaves
falling near the tree for shelter—
Here we will spend the night
little sister. Here we light the fire
for supper. No we will not burn.

In Memoriam

Partly, if I remember—
oak blooming yellow dust,
the flowers had not fallen—
in our yard, in Dorothy's,
doves mourning, the buzzsaw
down in the woods—this day
they cut the road through,
a red, muddy opening.

It was more like many days,
a month, they had it done;
we walked the dog to the end
of the street, to the thin
line of trees, and then
to the red roadbed—
like some ancient monument
carved, two banks like legs
spread, the road a snarled tongue.

On the walk back we lost
the tree where the names
were carved, the patch of vine,
the rotted log. The dog flushed
a squirrel, a feral cat, a crow—
the dog's running, a wagging happy
movement to kill that went unnoticed
as we went back up the hill to home.

Where My Father Is Buried I Have Not Been

That place withdrawing with the late sun
I long for, but cannot go *(It's too far, I'm too busy)*.
There, grey stone shadows the light, the light
too pale to keep the etched words clear, words
now blurring to granite, granite fading into grass,
all fading into the soft dark that always comes.

I imagine it is difficult for the bones to get used
to disappearing, the lift of wind so hard to navigate,
to be tumbled like a stone being polished or
a weed being torn from its root, polished until
there is only shine, torn until there is only dust,
and even those bright bits swallowed black.

How the night is made of these particles,
touching us, yet we cannot see them. And all
the questions remain: Why is he wearing
his raincoat in my mother's dreams. Where is he
going, has he gone. The particles form and disperse,
form and disperse. What do we know: an evening
wind curls in, ruffles the grass like fingers.
I only hope he can find home when he needs it,
knows us when he sees us.

Grace Confusing

Willow cherries bloomed too early pink,
the soft air made us foolish—
I fell to my knees spading dirt,
laid seed, fingered worms just started.
Shouldn't trees have known the frost
would soon come back, lick the blossoms brown,
bite my Impatiens' sprouts clean off, crisp
the worms to purple curls along the walk,
just bits to sweep aside. I wonder how trees
know anything: how do they conclude
flowers or leaves, what color or when.
Nothing seems to know, even the rapid sky
rambles clouds or rain, hurricanes or balmy wind—
even you slipped away unanswerably,
like a change in the weather or the dog chasing
the falling brown petals, spring too early chasing winter.

Gone to Brightness

Each leaf already wounded
at summer's edge, sun tips
white where green disappears
to sky. In that evaporating
place, someone's hands find
perfect tender, offer hope
for always spring—A prayer
always unfinished, opening—
like lips or red peonies
nodding in rain, or like
a high crag where moss blooms—
in the same voice forever,
as if you were still soft and new,
and unfinished could tell what word
would call back your bright disappearance.

Like Air

And so, her hair flips in the wind,
and so, even her skin
is only a window being raised.

Across the parking lot, small trees
burn in the sun, her feet lift
off the ground, no one knows

how close the dead are to us,
how leaves hurry to earth
too, how in her wheelchair

she can feel their soft hands,
veiny, dark, the brush of kelp,
that deep forest, where she can walk

again. Like the sun rushes
into a room, like where her
brush rests, the lace, who

will find her some afternoon
not sleeping anymore, not even
breathing, the window wide open.

To that Pilgrim Sky the Sun Slips

Cards fan oriental orange black white
across the daughter's back unfolding in the loose silk
her father brought from China years ago—
that her mother never wore, that never was
slipped across an elbow, never hemmed
or stitched to suit that long, once slim-
hipped once girl he wanted to please, wanted
to carry off to China. She never went, slubbed
fabric of those small worms folded deep in
her wooden chest heavy with material
she meant to sew, but never did get to—
yet other dresses were made: tide blue hibiscus
polished cotton A-line tent, herringbone tweed
wool jumper, white pique rickrack-trimmed empire:
each one daylight, wide fields of highland sheep
or river-plain cotton, places deep in her bones,
pulsed in her blood in the same rhythmic stitching
of her Singer—so much threaded, safe, trimmed
and finished, closeted in their good wood
Maryland house, so far from any China.
Now not even the fabric is left, silk gone to Good Will,
machine to the Methodists. No more sewing,
she couldn't remember how, and now he's died,
that distance unraveling, never traveled.

Bright Forgetting

Most of what is there is not remembered—
the ivy leaves, the box turtles, the oaks' grey bark—
mostly fallen, lost, browning to empty spaces.
As if those woods stand at the end of a sentence…
incorrect, rotting away,
and even the blue sky seems wrong, holds only mourning doves or
chickadees, no proper words to close the day.

Each time I visit you, I touch your grey hair, touch my own greying,
wonder what else is gone—a gold bracelet, a ring,
the woman next door, or your last best friend.
Your blue eyes pale with all this missing.
Your temples veined with ghosts.
Each time I come, the door is opened wider,
the window filled with birds.
The cat on the bed purrs, its comfort your afghan, the birds,
the spot of sun.

In that brightness, we just go blind.
Your eyes only half see the cat, the darting birds.
Light infuses the macular so it cannot see the center.
Only the periphery is left—
a few acquaintances, the suit you made him, a cracked porch step,
the cackling of your mother's chickens,
the stand of trees at the edge of town bending green
then gold then almost white in a hard wind one early fall.

In the Same Boat

They call me, asking for money, and I do not know what to say,
so I say what is best, anything, just leave me alone, the dog barking
so loud, can't they hear, sun slipping behind, slowly clouds
shape into black telephones, rain again, long wires of it down, yard
no longer speaking, just red mud, shards of grass, my house leans in

when will it start taking water, how long do we have—
Mother's house always tight as a drum, trimmed out, she sailed
green as the oak canopy, with flourish of azalea, ivy over the yardarm,
stern of patio, bow of screen porch, the quay of rock wall, decks
polished floorboards, wall to wall carpet, slip-covers, curtains

all by her hands, each stitch so tight—my father, my sister, me—
and now her grandchildren and her grandchildren's children call me
asking, while their boats go bobbing, rocking, slipping under the waves—
what can I do, what can she do, she says, *nothing,*
they must stand on their own feet. But none have their sea legs,
even my father has drowned and my sister floats underground—

no one to rescue anyone—
Doctors say *six to eight glasses of water per day,*
this will heal you. I stand with my cup full,
one grackle madly slapping water out of the birdbath,
while the stray white dog at the street laps rain from the gutter,
and clouds stoop to lazily finger the tarmac, feather the curb,
bruise the last bits of lawn again and again,
water filling the last supposed chipmunk hole.

Domestica

Dogs know who I am, their skin shedding fur,
hair swirling across the red-brick linoleum.
When I go to see important people
they see how important fur is to me,
how I decorate my very professional calendar book,
my coat, the seat of my pants, my good sweater with it.
I make a statement and hair spits out, or some lonely
howl. This is how the house sounds, the rough growls
of play, the hungry talk, the pleading yelps to be let out.
Always begging begging for food.

Imagine the pack wide for the hunt, tails straight out—
each molecule of wind telling them how to find the herd,
each blade of grass pointing the way—the deermice,
voles, the prairie hens stay hidden, still—those fourleggeds
can hear blood pumped too loud, or breath when it slips
too hard. They know how the heart tastes and the bones.

My sister keeps a dog she's scared of, throws it treats
so it won't bite, keeps it so it might bite others.
The dog doesn't know where it is, who is alpha,
who is not, from where the next kill will come.
Curled in an old quilt at night, it eats kibble, then
downs a young deer, dragging a leg or something home,
most left uneaten, rotting somewhere in the woods.

Now with the dog, she keeps her son, forty years old
and dying. His grey breath falling on every knickknack,
the particles of his skin make the dog cry. Nothing
I do or say is right. Only howling will do. Hairs stick
to my skin, my bones, I know that pack will soon be done—
the son will die, the dog move on, my sister I don't know.
When the moon comes full, it might hold her tears,
but not her bitterness. She will not call to me, nor I to her.

Each pack must have a home. Each to its own desire—
a cave or sheltered place. When the members go out to hunt,
they leave the pups with an older dog, so-called "uncle" or "aunt."
Mostly mice are what they eat, even some seeds
and grass. But when the plain fills with a herd,
or the clearing a small group of deer, the pack must go.

I go hunting some good steaks or chicken for dinner,
the grocery so bright, everything shiny—only at home,
my dogs whine. Even when it's frozen, they know
the taste of blood, remember the moving animal,
the slaughter and return, the dance of family feeding,
no words for grace.

Duende: For Her
> *Nobody knows you. No. But I sing of you.* —Frederico Garcia Lorca

Dark fluted clouds drag across the sky,
bound where, in what kind of wind—
No te conoce nadie. No. Pero yo te canto.
I want to speak about your smile,
want to keep the moon from blotting out
the stars, the sun-cut lines of your skin,

the jut of your chin and high cheekbones,
the faded flowers of your dress.   I want
to touch your hands, the knot of each knuckle,
the veins fat on thin, tan skin,
to see you gardening, not buried,
not gone like the geese he gave you—
those white and grey girls who ran
to only your scatter of seed,
biting, hissing at anyone else.

Today, not even one goose or hen remains,
no fig tree blooms in the side yard,
no porch swing arches up and back
in the stark light of one low hanging bulb.
Now, no matter how much I remember,
your arms cannot hold me, your flock arrows
some other sky.   All things migrate—
a son has a table, a daughter a chair,
but soon not even they
will have a stick to tether you.

Soon, who will be able to tell
how you held the egg basket,
the raccoon gun, the burlap sack, the hoe,
how you moved from row to row weeding.
Now strawberries in the field rot in summer heat,
sweet biscuits go unmade, the beans go hard,
tomatoes black, and rows of corn

fall to the crows at morning.
No day knows you anymore:
the moon does its work while we are sleeping

Forgetting comes too easily,
I cannot hold who you were—
the fishpole goes missing, the tin pail,
and how far it is to the pond
hidden deep in the meadow,
beyond the rise, before the stand of oaks—
what shadows are waiting,
waiting for the fish to rise, waiting for stars to scatter like seed
across the hazy just dark sky.

Light Lifting

My father must be now a star, a pinprick against
night, light so far away it may be gone, and yet
I think I see it, hope he is there, even if unspeaking,
transformed, dim. Even now our old dog is crying,
half-howls, his own odd speech to tell me
let me out, let me in, feed me, lift me up to walk—
hips weak, he is no longer able to lift himself.
So I lift him, lay towels across the slick floor, and
he is able to go out. Who among us would not lift the dying,
even when that height is more than we can bear,
the upswing of heaviness toward nothing, more than
we can think. How my dog is like my father. My father
like the dog, poor-hipped—his hip shattered from a fall,
with bones too soft to hold the pins, the doctors simply
cut the bone away. That bone buried a month and then
he followed. Our husky may do the same—follow a bone,
find himself running, hip-free, in some bright place
I can barely see.

Countless

Several Keck Twin astronomers search for the long lost stars
like parents hoping the child will be found, even while its photo-
copy faces tear away, ink streaking down telephone poles.
So they try with the radio telescope too. It is so hard to find
that long ago light that they stay up late, eat bad takeout food,
nod off by the computer screen that remembers every photograph
ever taken. How the child becomes part of the family—
so smart, so stupid, so pretty, so clumsy—its small, five pointed
hands in futile signals to reveal an earlier compass, a shifted map.
I could not say how you were lost, how I imagined I held you
even when your hair might fall away or your tiny cries told me
it was too far to come. Now I peer through the telescope even
in the bright day. I think I see how the bird becomes part of the tree,
its wings leaves, the heart wind, light bones nodding branches—
the very thing we look for hidden in what we already see.

Looking Up

Blackness found us last night
turned with bits of light—
stars gone a thousand years,
still spinning into our poor lensed
telescope rotated up, then up again.

So much sky, deep and far,
all that light tumbling upside down:
headless king, lady in a chair,
seven sisters pale and dreaming,
and the white dog barking endlessly—

As if those fiery pinpricks
had a pattern, made a shape,
a story they are still telling—
unsettled or disappeared,
where are they going,
where did they go,
how do the stories end.

You take the compass out
to find them, a chart
to hold the sky that rises
so wide I trip at the edge
of the deck to see, almost
another falling.

Not Yet Easeful

Whatever it is it won't come easily,
not yet anyway. Yesterday she
would say patience, say wait, say
come, let's go on now, but that
was the other life, the one slipping
away like a trailing conversation,
or the way voices clump together
at the train station, how they fade
to pindots, to nothing as he waves
leaving or returning—Which way is he
going, now dead like he is, but he keeps
coming back—once crawling, then flying,
next slumped by the tree, his legs like roots
following the ground, finding it, sad
as a willow, rutted as an oak—he must
think she understands, she is listening,
what will she say, what does she know—
she only admits that things aren't clear,
that she has no money, that the room is cold,
that even eating seems too much trouble,
while a full moon rises, lies down in shadows,
and trees fall across her bed.

What Trees Remember

Rising at the back of the house on a blue day,
a russet flame of oak, so bright it could be
speaking. But there are no translations,
the evening comes too soon, turns dark—

What I have in me that runs to the shadows
cannot speak. Whether unseen or just forgotten,
a black loam sprouts the blind white tips, almost green.
Even the full sun slips and seeks its hiding place.

My mother is afraid to die, so she dies in stages,
finds consolation in forgetfulness. Fading, she does
not know what she is losing, but I do. I want to hear
those days again, the plain-spoken embrace of dinners

ready on the wooden table, of clean sheets pegged
to the line, of shirts made, mended, washed, and ironed
again and again. This litany now abandoned branches,
leaves gone to ground, the sky still and wider than before.

Field in Late Summer

Even as she measures the empty field with her fingertips spread,
his footprints, once pitted in clay, are disappearing, already
his name has fallen away, over barbed wire, to the ragweed,
beyond the last tufts of cotton left in the furrows, to clouds swerving
beyond the cortex, the sound of his breathing shallower, rain

clotting into every memory, every thought. As if she could
do something, could have done, near the end of the field,
the edge where goldfinches light on nodding sunflowers, where
the unseen parts of days shudder
like the small yellow and black wings.

Black walnut, hickory, oak shadow the gate, the creek over the rise,
its vein a pulse tucked deep in skin.
An early moon disregards the rain, the trailing clouds, the past.
No one will be coming in for dinner,
the porchlight so dim, the swing's slats shining, empty.
Each small stroke like fireflies, a bright forgetting.

Heard While Still Sleeping

Asleep in the afternoon, green car blurring across the Utah desert,
my father and mother silhouetted on the front seat, unspeaking,
I fell into the desert's dream,
my father's elbow reddening on the window edge,
cactus, tumbleweed, all the surprising birds and bits of water,
even cattails that knife upright against the wide sweep of heat,
shadow the mottled snakes and quail.

There is no photograph: the long hours in those dreams,
heat-drugged, skin patterned in the backseat vinyl weave,
the rest stop interruptions.
Documentation goes later: snaps of California cousins,
picnic food on a checked tablecloth, the amusement park tour,
first dip in the Pacific.
But before the destination, and far from home,
far from east coast white oaks and hills hiding sky,

jackrabbits dart from the bluestem,
turtles stretch their necks in the sun:
the hidden life elbows in as if it were speaking:
stories stretch for miles, stories I want to remember:
how the coyote dances for the kangaroo mouse,
the mouse's small chest heaving,
how the cactus might be waving its arms,
how my father laughs, and Mother squints in the brightness,
the car still speeding toward the motel, the pool,
the clean white sheets.

Canyon Tour

It looked like an O-K, fingers circled as if holding a penny,
something coppery, shiny, surrounded in flesh, or perhaps
like a bowl, observed from a certain angle, full of honey,
or, no, a hand cupped to catch sweet tea spilled—millennia since
something had fallen, something was saved—sun burnished a granite
outcrop, thrust up sediment, Pleistocene rising—

Park Ranger O'Brien's red hair is mostly what we remember
as she explains the Quaternary periods, the Havasupai, how little
it rains, her hair furrowing, shimmery like the canyon,
so many different reds.
She pops up in my dreams back home, thigh-deep in water,
explaining why the Indians are leaving, why the fence is built,
why some rocks keep changing into other things, even into people.

When I first heard you say okay, was I riding the small blue bike,
breaking free from your hold, or was I crossing the creek log,
now rotted, gone, or finding the knife or bowl
on our neighborhood walk on some long gone Saturday,
and was the last time in my kitchen, when you said
that easy word again, your trembling, veiny hands breaking the glass:
O'Brien is telling us now, it's okay, walk to the edge
see how the ocean rises, recedes,
how water leaves rocks the color of hair or blood.

Out of Coeur d'Alene

Grey blue river snakes through bright green,
the full sun fingers each blade, the wind, the wind
breathes in the morning air, breaking fast,
the oxygen meal, brightness rushing with the water,
the petticoat foam, the ruts of granite and deep pools,
long legs of pebble and brown sand—this dance
bending the earth, zippering hills, whirling over the falls
to find the salmon, the scavenger eagle, the spring
ravenous bear, its skin motley and scarred.

How can we follow this river, find that falling life
that knows what is prey, what is predator,
that knows the particular stir of each wind,
that knows how to eat rock, slowly slowly,
and finally how to disappear into its own vast deep:
Traveling west when I was ten, we rode along a river
mineral green like our car, like a tv screen—
the hills turned to strip-mine sand,
the sun just glare, every color burning to white:
Death, they say, falls like night, but since you died,
I feel it rush and swerve like the river into each day,
foam so bright it eats everything away.

Going into the Grand Canyon

An empty moon, stars hollow across the sky, the things we knew
no longer stick or fill up anywhere—everywhere light empties,
falls away, dark rising across the canyon wall,
reds, yellows, oranges gone so quickly, so soon. Too soon.
It seems everyone will die: where once there was hope or astrology,
now it's only numbers. The road that goes to an ocean,
just dry, cracked two-lane here, a rut where things go missing.

As we go down in the canyon, it just gets hotter, with less water;
if our children knew us, it would not be so dark; if anyone we knew
could stay, the sun might not go dim each day,
clouds blurring without rain. No one knows what death is—
cliffs rise up with no explanations, no inventions.
Each outcrop and cave mouths nothing. Not even red paint hands
or antelopes tell any certain thing—
stories evaporate as soon as rain, the flesh sooner.

The pack is heavy, our shoes all dirt, sweat rimes salty layers—
this geography the skin knows: the body only trying to keep cool,
every operation, attribute, even the upright spine, the arched feet,
the hips, the blood's curved platelets, the heart protected
deep in the chest beating the walk's rhythm: every thing
to help us stay alive, the same bits and pieces that fall away,
like the pack flung wide, to save calories for the brain,
to save sweat for the heart, but always there is finally
nothing left to throw away to save ourselves—
the canyon floor waiting, its tiny river rushing deeper stronger
than all the people, dogs or children we have ever known.

Plain Song

I keep a plain inside myself that doesn't exist,
in my nine room house grass won't grow—
as if buffalo hulk between my shoulder-blades,
pronghorn dot the curve of my hip-bones,
a sloped Conestoga sticks to the ruts of my lungs,
and somehow slung in my arms and legs, faded green
and yellowed grasses edge rippling to blue—
as if that hidden wind has fingers and a piano tilts on the ridge,
as if the woman in the wagon is singing—
her skirt, not calico, but grey pleated cotton, dust-caked hem,
shoes a size too small, white blouse rimed with dry sweat,
her bones, like wagon ribs jutting in canvas skin—
but now no California, no lift of mountains:
the axle cracked, open to fever, the too bright day—
the belled curve of her tongue skims the last shimmering
notes of *shall we gather at the river*;
a Sioux shuffles toward the rig, sighs,
but he only asks a blessing from the Christian
to help him on his pilgrimage—
the mules go loose, her man never returns for the rescue,
even the sun rolls away, higher, louder—
I wait for the eggs to boil hard,
for the phone to ring, for the mail to come,
never see the Indian who might sidle in to watch tv—
dropseed, fescue, foxtail, grama, bluejoint, buffalo, wire, spear,
switch and bent grass stuck to his hair, his skin, his tired feet.

Where All Things are Made New

Each of us is moving to another country, even in winter's short light,
the moon eating the sun, night hovering on the horizon,
the sky pale silk: we carry gold with us and firewood,
the wool blankets and hardtack, books and beans,
mirrors and axes, our grandmothers' bibles,
and grease for the wagon wheels, to keep everything turning.

I don't know which of us will leave first, which of us will carry water
enough to get there, enough to keep there and drink in long cool gulps,
but there may be no need, for the streams are full and clear,
the salmon running, trout skimming the shore,
pines, oaks, maples, ironwood, and hawthorn

filtering noise and light to shape something that might tell us
where we are going next. Thousands walk there anyway,
without answers. One man climbs to the bluff, his body charring
slowly in the brightness, a shadow in the burn of sun.
At the crest, he may fall into himself, we may fall with him.
Mostly, what we want is worthless—the beads and lace,
the extra skillet, the trunk full of pictures—
these things we must throw over,
so we and the oxen can go the miles we have to go.

Departing

Now I have been where the wind blows the bones around,
rushes them into the blue cavern of sky, wears them down
to dust, then nothing, then to invisible things—
a place where graves sit like swing seats stuck in thistle
and seed-scattered dirt waiting for the green sprout—

there bright grey rutted bare oaks circle the hill, and the asphalt road
crosses it. Clouds roil then die; winter sun arches low,
yet widens the view:
from here sitting under the flapping cerulean plastic funeral tent,
I can see farther than that last vignette caught in late summer's heat:
my sister wearying my mother and father, how they ran to me
to tell me it wasn't true, even when I knew it wasn't,

even when I knew how she was, and remains. But now, my mother
rushes to my father; they run together, boneless and unweary,
through the upright oaks, skimming the road, like a happy wind
or a brush of air, while we stay to hear the minister
intone the final prayer, its slow and fetching meter, a harkening.
Then I see how the hill rolls down toward the river—

how the mudline widens, and the herons gather, still and brave,
while the dimming light floods the range of tree stumps, cattails,
and odd weeds. The whole world is turning toward night.
But when I go to say goodbye to my sister
and she hurries the other way,
I have a strange knowledge of how bright the darkness is.

Lynne Martin Bowman was The Comstock Review's National Chapbook Contest Winner for *Water Never Sleeps*. Also, she has been Sonora Review's Poetry Prize winner and Crab Orchard Review's Poetry Prize 2nd place. She was 2nd place in the NC Writers' Network's Campbell Poetry Book Award, received honorable mention in the Randall Jarrell Poetry Competition, and was twice Emily Dickinson Award finalist. Her work has appeared in *Southern Poetry Review, The Mississippi Review, The International Poetry Review, New Millennium Writings, Crosswinds, The Sow's Ear Poetry Review, Tar River Poetry, Pig Iron Press* among others.

Born in Maryland of Mississippi parents, she grew up in Chevy Chase. She graduated with a B.A. in English from Ohio Wesleyan University and then worked in Columbus for Franklin County's Social Services. She returned to school to earn an MFA in Creative Writing from Bowling Green State University (OH), won a Devine Fellowship, and taught at BGSU and Heidelberg University. She then earned a PhD in English from the University of North Carolina-Greensboro with a dissertation on the poet, Robert Bly. Rescued by two dogs and one cat, she and her husband live in Greensboro, NC.